SCHOOL JOKES FOR ALIENS

Also available by Scoular Anderson,
and published by Young Corgi Books:

MY FIRST JOKE BOOK

A–Z OF ANIMAL JOKES

THE SPIDER AND CHIPS JOKE BOOK

Scoular Anderson

School Jokes for Aliens

YOUNG CORGI

SCHOOL JOKES FOR ALIENS

A YOUNG CORGI BOOK 0 552 526657

First published in Great Britain by Young Corgi Books

PRINTING HISTORY
Young Corgi edition published 1991

This book is set in 14/16pt Baskerville
by Chippendale Type Ltd., Otley, West Yorkshire.

Young Corgi Books are published by Transworld Publishers Ltd., 61–63 Uxbridge Road, Ealing, London W5 5SA, in Australia by Transworld Publishers (Australia) Pty. Ltd., 15–23 Helles Avenue, Moorebank, NSW 2170, and in New Zealand by Transworld Publishers (N.Z.) Ltd., Cnr. Moselle and Waipareira Avenues, Henderson, Auckland.

Made and printed in Great Britain by Cox & Wyman Ltd., Reading, Berks.

Emma: When I got up this morning there was an aeroplane in my bedroom.

Eric: Why was that?

Emma: I left the landing light on.

Dougie: My dad beats me up every morning.

Donna: That's awful!

Dougie: Yes, he gets up at six and I get up at seven.

BREEP
Earthmode time 8.17
AGENT ZEB...PLEASE REPORT ON STRANGE HISSING NOISE...
Eleven forty-five

Knock, knock!
Who's there?
Buster.
Buster who?
Buster school.

Why did the boy take a car to school?

To drive the teacher up the wall.

What's the difference between a school teacher and a train?

One says: 'Spit out that gum immediately!' and the other says: 'Chew, chew, chew!'

What's the difference between a teacher and a railway guard?

One trains minds and the other minds trains.

How did the teacher keep her pupils on their toes?

She put drawing pins on their chairs.

Teacher: You should have been here at nine o'clock!

Kevin: Why, did I miss something?

REPORT: HOLOGRAPHIC FINGER SENSOR PRINT-OUT
OBJECT: SCHOOL-BAG, CONTENTS OF...

BLUE BIRO	COMB (PINK)	FIVE HANKIES
RED BIRO	DANDRUFF	THREE WATCHES ~ ALL BROKEN
LIPSTICK (RED)	SIX TEA-BAGS	PACKET OF TOFFEES
PERFUME (CALLED 'IRRESISTIBLE')	PURSE CONTAINING: TWENTY-ONE POUNDS, THIRTY-FIVE PENCE	33 HAIRPINS
NAIL FILE		ONE PAPERBACK
BUNCH OF KEYS	SET OF FALSE TEETH MARKED 'EATING'	ENTITLED 'DANCE
CHOCOLATE BISCUIT (HALF-EATEN)		OF THE ZOMBIES'
	SET OF FALSE TEETH MARKED 'SMILING'	48 BITS OF PAPER, FLUFF, GRIT, ETC...
CHEQUE BOOK		

Why did the teacher wear dark glasses?

Because her pupils were so bright.

Why is a classroom like a car?

Because it contains a lot of nuts and a crank up front.

Knock, knock!
Who's there?
Pencil.
Pencil who?
Pencil fall down if there's no elastic.

BREEP Earthmode time 9.51

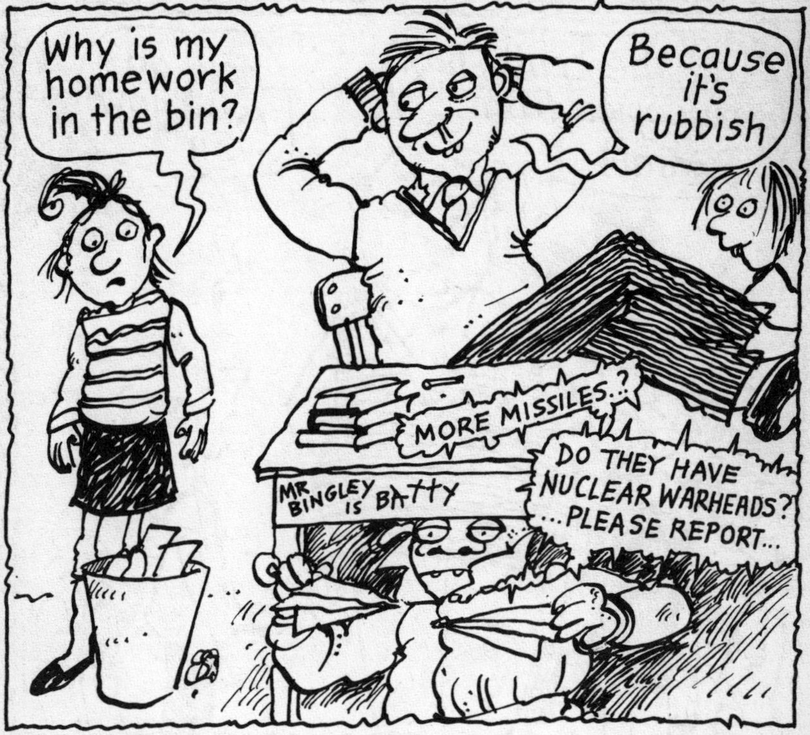

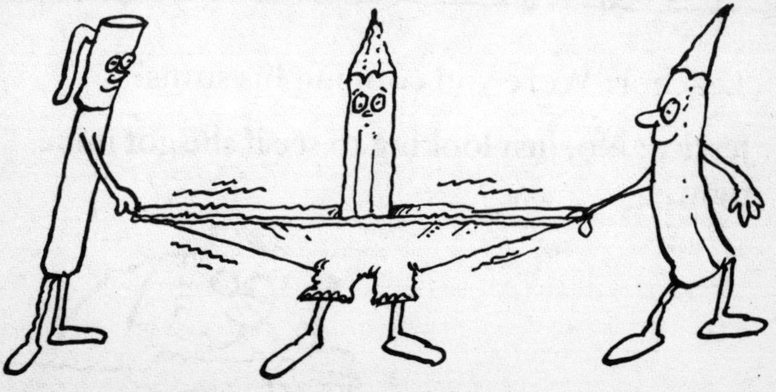

Teacher: Were you copying his sums?

Jessica: No, just looking to see if she got mine right.

Teacher: I hope I didn't see you cheating.

Amrit: I hope you didn't too, Miss!

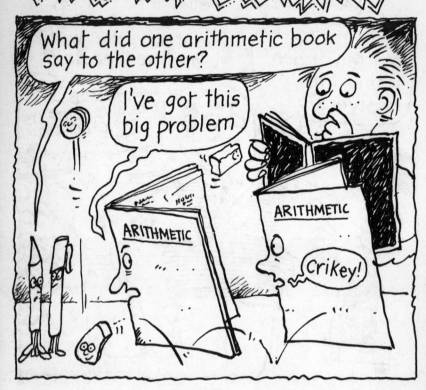

Teacher: Billy, did your homework questions give you any trouble?

Billy: No, but the answers did!

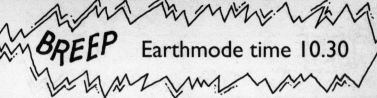

NOSTRIL-CLEANING CLOTHS (GRUBBY)	MUSICAL TAPE ~ WALLY SLABSTONE'S GREATEST HITS	ANSWERS TO NEXT WEEK'S HISTORY TEST
RUBBER BANDS		
SWEETS	PIANO KEY (WHITE)	MARMALADE
CRISPS	PIANO KEY (BLACK)	TOAST (2 BITS)
SAWDUST	DOOR KEY (BENT)	GRIT, GRAVEL, FLUFF ETC.
DOG BISCUITS	FOOTBALL BOOT LACE	

BREEP BREEP

I wish I had been born a thousand years ago

why?

IMPORTANT DATES
1066 1561
1090 1566
1142 1507
1314 1508
1325 1522
1403 1527
1486 1603
1490 1604

Teacher: In 1492 Columbus found America.

Ellie: I didn't know it was lost, Sir!

Teacher: Lyndon, tell me something about the Iron Age.

Lyndon: I'm afraid I'm a bit rusty on that, Miss.

Teacher: What is air?

Wendy: A balloon with its skin off.

Teacher: What do you know about the Dead Sea?

Roddy: I didn't even know it was ill.

Teacher: Where is Felixstowe?

Laura: At the end of Felix's foot.

Teacher: Why did Henry VIII have so many wives?

Angela: Because he liked to chop and change.

BREEP BREEP BREEP
Earthmode time 11.00
NGA DINGA DINGA DING
AGENT ZEB... SPECIMEN TEACHER RECEIVED... PERHAPS SOME MISTAKE HERE... PLEASE CHECK...
AGENT ZEB...PLEASE REPORT ON LOUD RINGING NOISE...

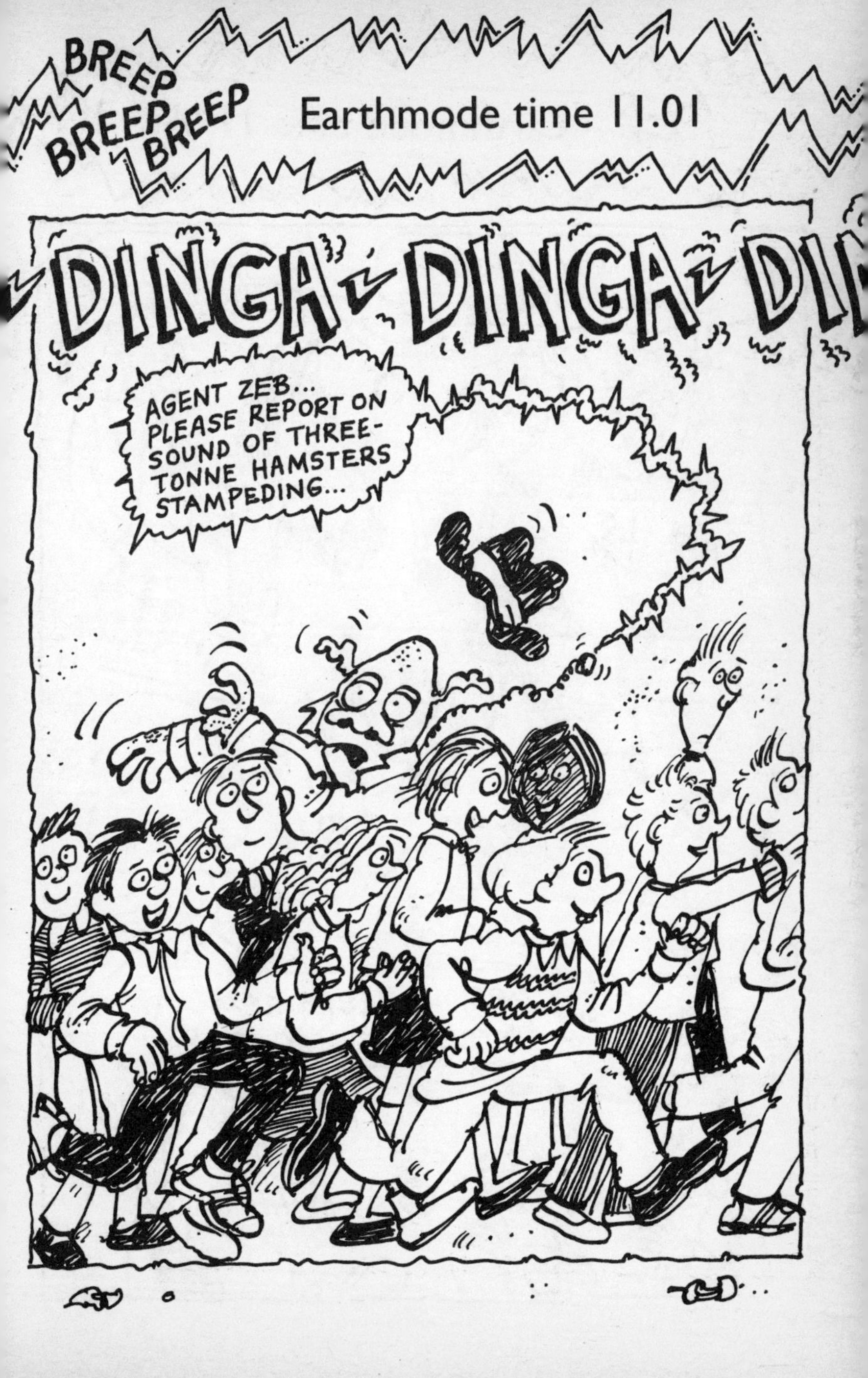

Hope: Our music teacher plays the piano by ear.

Holly: Don't her earrings get in the way?

Teacher: What do you call a small Indian guitar?

Clinton: A baby sitar.

Teacher: Gavin, what's the difference between a living song-writer and a dead one?

Gavin: One composes and the other decomposes.

BREEP Earthmode time 11.43

Music teacher: Now, Horace, what would you like to play?

Horace: Truant, Sir.

Why is history the sweetest lesson?

Because it's full of dates.

Why is a drama teacher like the pony express?

Because she's a stage coach.

Teacher: Adrian, what is a volcano?

Adrian: A mountain with hiccups.

Teacher: Yasmin, what's a fjord?

Yasmin: A Norwegian motor car.

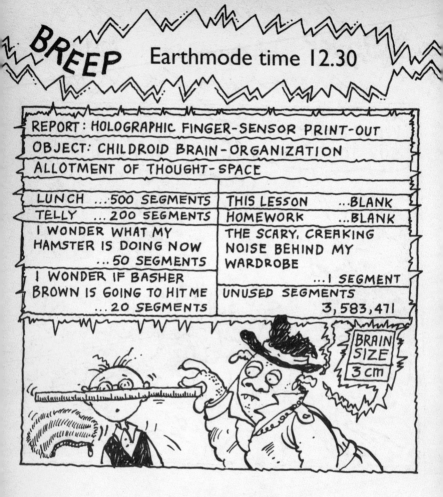

BREEP Earthmode time 12.30

REPORT: HOLOGRAPHIC FINGER-SENSOR PRINT-OUT

OBJECT: CHILDROID BRAIN-ORGANIZATION

ALLOTMENT OF THOUGHT-SPACE

LUNCH ...500 SEGMENTS	THIS LESSON ...BLANK
TELLY ...200 SEGMENTS	HOMEWORK ...BLANK
I WONDER WHAT MY HAMSTER IS DOING NOW ...50 SEGMENTS	THE SCARY, CREAKING NOISE BEHIND MY WARDROBE
I WONDER IF BASHER BROWN IS GOING TO HIT ME ...20 SEGMENTS	...1 SEGMENT
	UNUSED SEGMENTS 3,583,471

BRAIN SIZE 3 cm

Teacher: Which travels faster, heat or cold?

Angus: Heat, Sir, because you can catch cold!

Teacher: What does Hastings 1066 mean to you?

Brian: William the Conqueror's phone number?

BREEP BREEP
Earthmode time 12.45
NGA DINGA DING
AGENT ZEB... PLEASE REPORT ON REPEAT OF LOUD RINGING NOISE...

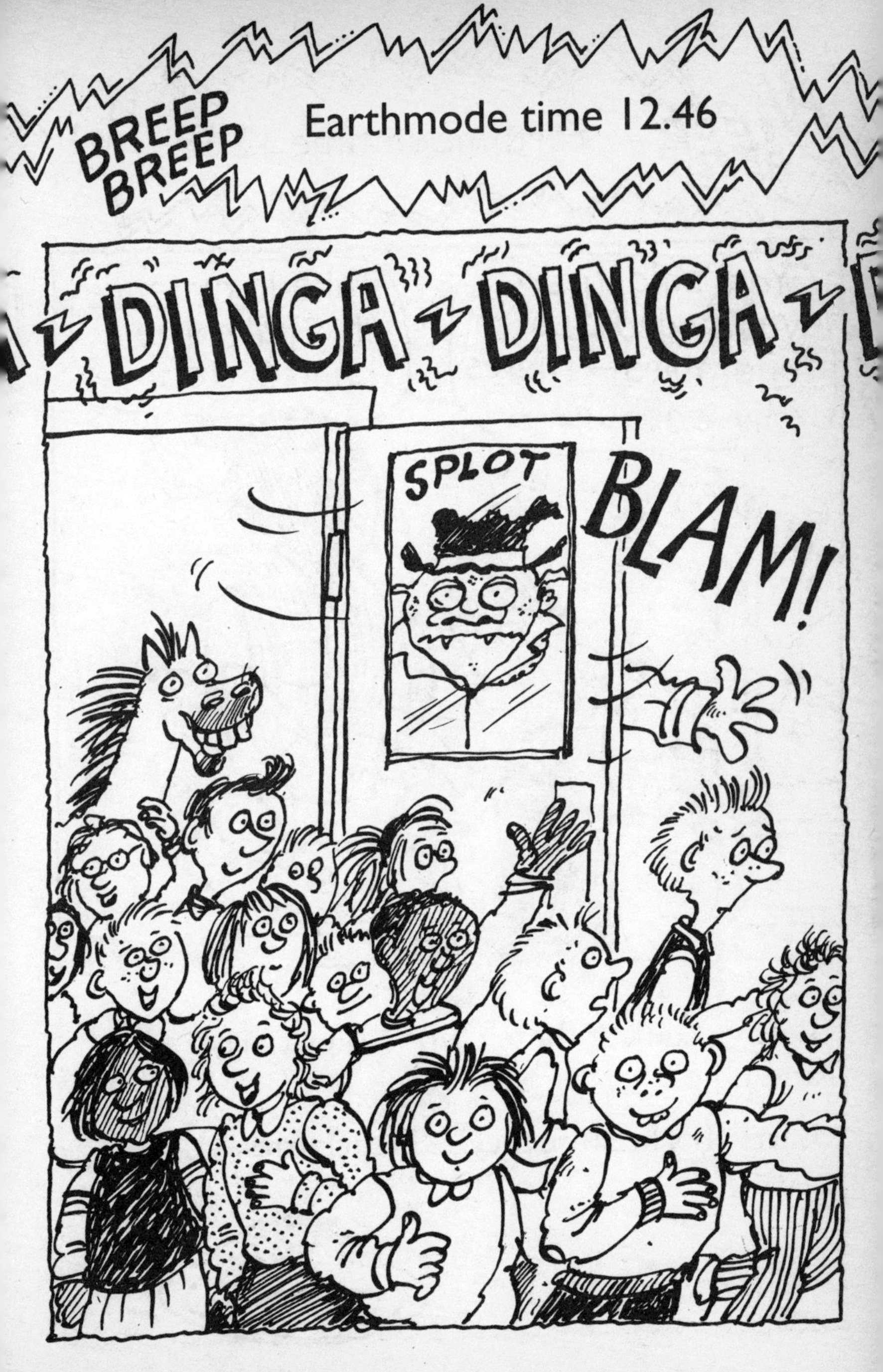
BREEP BREEP
Earthmode time 12.46
DINGA DINGA
SPLOT
BLAM!

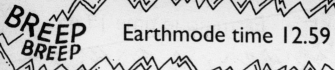

Leroy: Look at these chips — they're red, white and blue!

Barry: It's because they're French fries.

Poppy: There's a cockroach nibbling my hamburger!

Rachel: Don't worry they have very small appetites.

Ferdie: Will my hamburger be long?

Dinner lady: No, round as usual.

Audrey: Eat your spinach, it'll put colour in your cheeks.

Arlene: I don't want green cheeks!

Elton: Why are you having alphabet soup?

Elvis: So I can read while I'm eating!

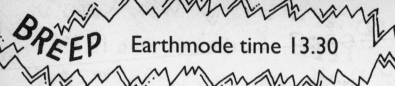

Why did the dinner lady get an electric shock?

She stood on a bun and a currant went up her leg!

What lives in a plastic box and hangs around belfries?

The Lunch pack of Notre Dame.

Fatima: Why did Eddie swallow 50p?

Freida: It was his dinner money.

Marlene: How do you swim 100 metres in two seconds?

Melanie: Don't know.

Marlene: Swim over a waterfall!

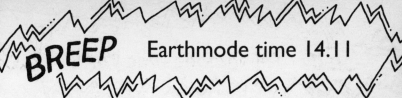

Warren: Why can't Robin play cricket?

Walter: Because he's lost his bat, man.

Shelley: Why do you call your goalkeeper Cinderella?

Susie: Because she's always **running away from the ball.**

What did one pencil say to the other?

I've got a lead ache.

REPORT: CONTINUED

OBJECT: TEACHER'S CUPBOARD, CONTENTS OF

1 STALE CHRISTMAS PUDDING	3 SCHOOL PANTO ANIMAL SUITS (DUCK, RAT, BLUE WHALE)
1 BOTTLE BRONZO SUN TAN OIL	EDDIE'S LUCKY ALLIGATOR TOOTH
BOX OF PUNISHMENT LINES BY PUPILS (7,583,705 LINES IN TOTAL)	
	SMALL COLONY OF BATS
10 WATER PISTOLS	1 MOUSE SKELETON
1 FOLDING CHAIR	GRAVEL, COBWEBS ETC. ETC.

Why did the cross-eyed teacher have trouble with his class?

He couldn't control his pupils.

I've come to collect my Janine. She's got a dental appointment

CRACK!

Why do young witches always get A in English?

Because they're good at spelling

Wanna be bookends?

SCRUNCH

Which American state produces the most pencils?

Pennsylvania.

Teacher: What sort of clothes did they wear during the Great Fire of London?

Tommy: Blazers, Miss.

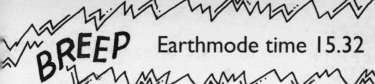

Imelda: What does the 'O' mean on your test paper?

Marlon: I think it's a moon. The teacher ran out of stars.

BREEP
BREEP
BREEP
Earthmode time 15.45
INGA-DINGA-DI
AGENT ZEB...

Ella: Your spelling isn't very good.

Eric: What do you mean? These are my sums!

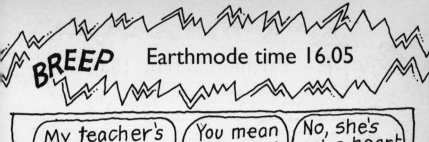

BREEP Earthmode time 16.05

Lloyd: Can I hold your hand?

Lucy: No thanks, it's not heavy.

Steven: Are you coming out to play?

Joey: No, I'll have to help Dad with my homework.

Lana: How are your exam marks?

Alison: They're underwater.

Lana: What do you mean?

Alison: Below C level!

If you would like to receive a Newsletter about our new Children's books, just fill in the coupon below with your name and address (or copy it onto a separate piece of paper if you don't want to spoil your book) and send it to:

**The Children's Books Editor
Transworld Publishers Ltd.
61–63 Uxbridge Road
Ealing
London W5 5SA**

Please send me a Children's Newsletter:

Name: ....

Address: ....

....

....

All Children's Books are available at your bookshop or news-agent, or can be ordered from the following address:
Transworld Publishers Ltd.
Cash Sales Department,
P.O. Box 11, Falmouth, Cornwall TR10 9EN

Please send a cheque or postal order (no currency) and allow 80p for postage and packing for the first book plus 20p for each additional book ordered up to a maximum charge of £2.00 in UK.

B.F.P.O. customers please allow 80p for the first book and 20p for each additional book.

Overseas customers, including Eire, please allow £1.50 for postage and packing for the first book, £1.00 for the second book, and 30p for each subsequent title ordered.